# the art of convection

Published by Jenn-Air, a division of Maytag Appliances
Recipe Development: Jill Means and Deborah Vickers Wagman
Design: Scott Severson
Photography and Styling: Wagman & Wagman
Editors: Jill Means and Karen Davis
Text © Maytag Appliances 2003
Photography © Bruce Wagman Photography, Inc.
Design © Maytag Appliances 2003

# contents

Lasagne with Shrimp, Scallops
and Snow Crab
see page 48

Cooking is the deepest of the arts of living. It touches us more profoundly than any other ritual.

We at Jenn-Air believe that with this statement, the masterful chef Jacques Pepin defined what is surely at the very core of the motivation, enthusiasm and devotion of passionate cooks.

It's about the art. About the art and craft we practice because we want to, not because we have to.

It is at the core of our insistence on beautiful, fresh ingredients. Of our arriving at the farmer's market before the dew has dried from the grass. Of our return-from-vacation suitcases stuffed with oils and vinegars instead of souvenirs and t-shirts. Of our groaning cookbook shelves and addiction to cooking classes.

It is also at the core of the tools we choose to practice our art and our craft.

At the core of why we keep our imported knives at razor sharpness. Of why we treasure our pans, the expensive ones, the heavy ones that gleam just so in the light. Or why we must have French porcelain soufflé dishes, seasoned maple chopping blocks and marble pastry boards.

And it is at the core of the oven we have chosen to use. This one.

The Jenn-Air® Oven with Multi-Mode™ Convection.

We pour so much into the meals that we prepare. So much time. So many special ingredients. So much of ourselves.

We need our oven to deliver on our expectation for perfection. And this oven does.

Roasted Vegetable Soup
see page 10

# starters

The first course for a special family dinner.

Scrumptious finger foods to accompany cocktails or wine.

Meals in and of themselves.

The Jenn-Air Multi-Mode™ Convection Oven makes them happen.

Click an everyday meal up a notch with an unexpected appetizer. Impress your party guests with a savory selection of hot hors d'oeuvre. Provide an impromptu post theatre repast for family and friends.

All it takes is your creativity and an oven that thinks like you do.

Jenn-Air Multi-Mode™ convection.

Let your creativity shine.

TIPS

When planning hors d'ouevre for a party, think balance. Serve something spicy with something cool. Serve one thing light with one thing rich. One crisp to one smooth. A healthy with a decadent.

The larger the group, the more food preferences come into play. Do not forget vegetarians, people with shellfish allergies or those on low cholesterol diets. They will thank you for it.

Choose a menu mix of dishes that are more difficult to prepare along with some that require nothing more than a striking arrangement on a serving dish. An assortment of whole cheeses or artisan breads are always beautiful and welcome additions to a buffet.

How much to make? Before a meal, a choice of 5-6 starters, allowing 1-2 per guest. When hors d'oeuvre are the meal, offer 8-10 choices, allowing 2-3 per guest.

# asiago crisps

*These crunchy rounds are as versatile as they are impressive. In addition to standing alone as appetizers, try them as a flavorful garnish for a mixed green salad, or floating atop tomato soup. They may also be made with Parmesano Reggiano or Pecorino Romano cheese.*

### ingredients

1 1/2 cups finely grated Asiago cheese
3 ounces Boursin cheese, softened
1/2 pint fresh raspberries

### preparation

Preheat oven to Convect Bake 375 degrees F.

Line a large baking sheet with a Silpat or other reusable nonstick bakeware liner.

Drop 1 level tablespoon of Asiago cheese into mounds 3 inches apart on baking liner. With fingers, spread to form each mound into a circle approximately 2 inches in diameter.

Convect Bake Asiago rounds until their edges just begin to color, for 6 to 7 minutes. Transfer crisps, still on bakeware liner, to wire rack; cool 2 minutes. Transfer to paper towels to absorb excess fat. Repeat with remaining Asiago cheese.

Place small dollops of Boursin cheese on top of each Asiago circle. Garnish with halved fresh raspberries.

Serves 12.

# roasted garlic with rosemary and point reyes blue cheese

*Garlic is the catsup of intellectuals.*

### ingredients

6 whole heads garlic
3 tablespoons butter, cut into small pieces
1/4 cup extra virgin olive oil
1 1/2 cups chicken broth
1/4 cup dry white wine
2 teaspoons chopped fresh rosemary
3 sprigs of fresh rosemary
6 ounces Pt. Reyes blue cheese, crumbled
2 warm baguettes, sliced into 1 inch rounds

### preparation

Cut 1/2 inch off the sprout end of each garlic head. Remove any loose papery skin. Place garlic cut side up in a baking dish. Top each with 1/2 tablespoon butter. Pour the oil over the garlic. Add chicken broth and wine to the bottom of the dish. Sprinkle chopped rosemary over the garlic. Place the rosemary sprigs in the the dish with the broth mixture.

Convect Roast, uncovered, at 375 degrees F. for 60 minutes, basting twice. Check halfway through roasting time, adding more broth if needed to maintain some sauce in the dish.

Sprinkle cheese over garlic, then continue baking an additional 5 minutes. Discard rosemary sprigs. Serve warm with sliced French bread for dipping.

Serves 15 as an hors d'oeuvre.

# roasted vegetable soup

(Photograph page 6)

*Only the pure of heart can make a good soup.*
Ludvig von Beethoven

### ingredients

2 medium yellow onions, quartered
3 large carrots, peeled and cut into large chunks
2 large parsnips, peeled and cut into large chunks
2 medium baking potatoes, peeled and quartered
5 ripe plum tomatoes, halved
3 cloves garlic
1 tablespoon olive oil
1/2 teaspoon salt
1/2 teaspoon freshly ground pepper
1/4 pound fresh green beans, stemmed
4 cups vegetable broth
2 teaspoons dried oregano
2 teaspoons dried basil
1 (28 ounce ) can whole tomatoes, chopped, reserve liquid

### preparation

Combine first nine ingredients in a baking dish. Toss to coat evenly with oil. Convect Roast at 425 degrees for 20 minutes. Add green beans to pan. Return to oven and Convect Roast an additional 20-30 minutes or until vegetables are tender.

Combine broth, oregano, basil, tomatoes and reserved liquid in a large saucepan. Bring to a boil, then reduce to simmer.

In batches, puree roasted vegetables in blender or food processor and process to smooth. Add to broth mixture.

Heat together 5 minutes to meld flavors, then serve hot.

Serves 8.

# roasted yellow pepper soup

The Mediterranean yellow color of this soup makes it a perfect choice as the first course for a late summer dinner. With its rich, mellow flavor, it will be appreciated year around.

### ingredients

1 medium red potato, peeled and cut into 1-inch cubes
2 stalks celery, coarsely chopped
1 carrot, peeled and coarsely chopped
1 small onion, peeled and coarsely chopped
1 clove garlic, minced
6 sweet yellow bell peppers, seeded and
  cut into 1-inch chunks
2 tablespoons extra virgin olive oil
6 cups chicken stock
1 teaspoon green peppercorns
1 cup heavy cream
salt and pepper to taste
8 leaves of fresh basil

### preparation

Place potato, celery, carrot, onion, garlic and yellow bell pepper pieces in a large roasting pan or baking sheet with 1-inch sides. Drizzle with olive oil. Convect Roast at 400 degrees F. for 35-40 minutes, or until almost tender. Set aside to cool slightly, approximately 5 minutes.

In a large soup pot, bring chicken stock to a boil. Stir in green peppercorns. Reduce heat to simmer.

In batches, puree the roasted vegetables in a blender or food processor until smooth. As each batch is pureed, stir it into the simmering chicken broth. Stir in heavy cream and mix well. Add salt and pepper to taste. Do not allow soup to boil. Serve immediately with fresh basil leaf garnish.

Serves 8.

Mozzarella, Tomato and
Roasted Yellow Pepper Salad
see page 15

# salads

With Jenn-Air® Multi-Mode convection, you are the artist.

An artist unfettered by the mundane problems of oven unpredictability.

An artist that demands—and gets—precise control over oven results.

Composed salads are your canvas for culinary color.

The Mediterranean hues of aromatic summer vegetables, convect-roasted to intensified sweetness. Fresh shrimp, convect-broiled to sizzling coral tenderness. Spring green asparagus quickly caramelized then spattered with lively tangerine accents.

A vibrant interplay of color, texture and pure nutrition, all on one plate.

When you paint with Jenn-Air® Multi-Mode convection,

your works are masterpieces.

## TIPS

To make sure that your greens are fresh and crisp, soak them in lukewarm water for 20 minutes. Spin or pat dry. Place several paper towels in the bottom of plastic bag, then loosely pack the bag with the greens. Refrigerate for several hours.

Coarsely chopped fresh herbs add another dimension of flavor to green salads. Choose them with abandon: your nose will always make a great choice.

The classic proportions for making your own vinaigrette are 3 parts oil to 1 part vinegar. If you use lemon or lime juice instead of vinegar, the proportions should be 4 parts oil to 1 part juice. With these formulas, you can create your own variations using your favorite vinegars and oils.

The darker the lettuce, the more vitamins and minerals it possesses.

Salad greens should be torn with the fingers, not cut with a knife. Knife cutting bruises lettuce and renders its internal structure incapable of absorbing water, which lessens crispness. The best tool for tossing salads is your hands.

Dressings, hot seafood, poultry and beef should be tossed into the salad at the very last minute.

# shrimp and black bean salad with papaya and key lime dressing

### ingredients

2 cups papaya, cubed
1/2 cup key lime juice
1/2 cup light olive oil
1 tablespoon minced garlic
1 tablespoon ground cumin
2 teaspoons cumin seeds
salt and freshly ground pepper to taste
1-15 ounce can black beans, rinsed and drained
2 avocados, pitted, peeled and cut into 1/2 inch cubes
1 large tomato, chopped
1 medium red onion, chopped
1/2 cup chopped fresh cilantro
20 large shrimp, peeled, deveined, tails removed

### preparation

Place rack in top position. Preheat oven to Convect Broil on HI.

To make dressing, combine papaya, lime juice, olive oil, garlic, cumin, cumin seeds, and salt and pepper in a food processor or blender. Process until smooth.

In large bowl, combine black beans, avocados, tomatoes, onion and cilantro. Add dressing and toss.

Broil shrimp 5-6 minutes, or until opaque. Add hot shrimp to rest of salad, toss well and serve immediately.

Serves 4.

# mozzarella, tomato and roasted yellow pepper salad

(Photograph page 12)

ingredients

2 large yellow peppers, halved and seeded
8 ounces fresh mozzarella cheese, sliced
2 large tomatoes, sliced
3 tablespoons fresh basil, coarsely chopped
1 tablespoon dijon mustard
2 tablespoons red wine vinegar
salt and ground pepper to taste
1 tablespoon water
1/3 cup extra-virgin olive oil

preparation

Convect Roast pepper halves at 400 degrees F. until skins begin to char and bubble, for approximately 30 minutes. Drop the hot peppers into a plastic bag, close, and let stand for 15 minutes. Remove the peppers and peel off their skin.

Arrange the cheese, tomatoes and peppers in an overlapping pattern on a serving dish and set aside.

With a wire whisk, beat together the basil, mustard, vinegar, salt, pepper, water and olive oil together until the mixture is smooth and creamy. Pour over the cheese, tomatoes and peppers. Serve at room temperature.

Serves 4.

# roasted asparagus salad with tangerine viniagrette

## ingredients

1 pound fresh asparagus, woody ends removed
1 tablespoon vegetable oil
2 large tangerines
1/3 cup tangerine juice (from 2 additional tangerines)
2 teaspoons rice vinegar
2 teaspoons sesame oil
2 teaspoons finely grated tangerine zest
1 clove garlic, minced
1 teaspoon grated fresh ginger
salt and freshly ground pepper to taste
green tops of 1 green onion, sliced very thinly on the diagonal
2 tablespoons toasted sesame seeds

## preparation

Wash asparagus and allow to soak in cool water for 15 minutes. Drain and pat dry with paper towels. Place in single layer in a 9x13 inch baking pan; drizzle with vegetable oil. Convect Roast at 450 degrees F. until just crisp-tender, about 15-17 minutes. Cool.

With a sharp paring knife, cut the peel and white pith from tangerines. Cut between membranes to release segments. Set aside.

In a small bowl whisk together the tangerine juice, vinegar, sesame oil, tangerine zest, garlic and ginger. Season with salt and freshly ground pepper to taste.

Combine asparagus and tangerine segments in a medium bowl.

Drizzle with tangerine dressing. Toss to combine. Sprinkle green onion tops and sesame seeds. Serve immediately.

Serves 4.

# arugula salad with clementines, roasted baby beets and gorgonzola

Arugula is also called rocket, roquette, and rucola. It is a bitter, peppery and mustardy green that is used frequently in Italy and is gaining popularity on American tables as well.

### ingredients

16 miniature, baby beets - Italian Chiogga beets, if available
1 teaspoon grated clementine zest
1 pound arugula, washed and dried
4 clementines, sectioned and seeded
1/3 cup crumbled Gorgonzola cheese
1/4 cup clementine juice
a grinding of fresh black pepper
1 tablespoon fresh lemon juice
2 teaspoons extra virgin olive oil
1/4 teaspoon salt
1/4 teaspoon Dijon mustard

### preparation

Trim beets, leaving one inch of root and one inch of stem. Scrub them very well and place them in a lightly oiled baking dish. Convect Roast at 425 degrees F. for 25-35 minutes, or until they pierce easily with the tip of a sharp knife. Do not peel and leave them whole. Set aside.

Combine clementine zest, arugula, clementine sections and Gorgonzola in a large bowl. In another bowl, whisk together the clementine juice, pepper, lemon juice, oil, salt and mustard.

Pour over salad mixture and toss to combine. Place salad mixture on serving plates, top with beets and serve immediately.

Serves 4.

Cottage Dill Loaves
see page 20

# breads

Crust and crumb.

Two elemental components of our most elemental of foods.

And, truly, the two parts of the loaf that depend more on the oven than they depend on you.

But with the Jenn-Air Multi-Mode Convection oven, you will be making artisinal quality bread—dense, grain—rich hearth loaves, crusty rounds of sourdough, fruit studded sweet buns, tender braided challas, scones and tea breads.

Breads with perfect crust and perfect crumb.

Create its flavors. Sponge it, proof it, raise it, knead it, and coddle it to your heart's content.

But when it is time to bake it, bake it with the Jenn-Air Multi-Mode Convection Oven.

TIPS

Unless you bake very frequently, it is best to keep whole grain flours such as rye or wheat in the refrigerator or freezer: they turn rancid quickly, especially in hot and humid climates. Simply pop the sack into a large zipping top bag for long term storage.

Give flour a few minutes to return to room temperature before adding to dough.

The wetter the dough, the larger the holes. This is an important thing to remember when attempting to duplicate European-style peasant breads. Try eliminating a quarter cup of flour each time you bake: gradually, you will become a pro at handling and forming softer loaves.

It can be hard to tell for sure if your bread is done. To take away the guesswork, just insert an instant-read thermometer into the center of the loaf. A temperature of 190-200 degrees indicates that the bread is ready.

# cottage dill loaves

(Photograph page 18)

The "herb decoupage" technique detailed in this recipe creates beautiful, showy loaves. It may be used with many different herbs on any shape, size or recipe of bread dough as well.

### ingredients

1 tablespoon active dry yeast
2 teaspoons sugar
1/4 cup warm water (110-115 degrees F)
1 cup low-fat cottage cheese, room temperature
1/2 cup finely chopped red onion
2 tablespoons chopped fresh dill
2 teaspoons dried dill seed
1 egg, lightly beaten
1 teaspoon salt
2 to 2 1/2 cups all-purpose flour
egg wash: 1 egg + 1 tablespoon water, beaten
large sprigs of fresh dill, whole

### preparation

In a large mixing bowl, dissolve the yeast and sugar in warm water. Let stand until foamy. Stir in the rest of the ingredients except for the egg wash and fresh whole dill. Mix well to form a soft dough. Turn dough out onto a lightly floured surface and knead until pliable and elastic. Place dough in an oiled bowl, cover with plastic wrap and allow to raise until double in bulk, about 1 1/2 hours.

Divide dough into 2 pieces. Shape each piece into a smooth round. Place rounds on two parchment paper-lined baking sheets. Brush heavily with egg wash. Gently apply whole dill sprigs to the tops of the loaves (they will stick to the egg glaze) Brush egg wash over the dill sprigs again, making sure that the dill sprigs are adhering to the loaves. Allow loaves to rise for an additional 30-45 minutes.

Preheat oven to Convect Bake 350 degrees F.

Convect Bake loaves for 25-27 minutes, or until a thermometer inserted into the center reads 190 degrees.

Cool slightly before slicing.

Serves 12 per loaf.

# vanilla scented challa

## ingredients

1 cup warm water
2 tablespoons active dry yeast
pinch of sugar
1/2 cup honey
1/3 cup melted butter
2 teaspoons pure vanilla extract
1/2 teaspoon salt
1 vanilla bean, halved lengthwise
4 large eggs, lightly beaten
5-6 cups bread flour
egg glaze: 1 egg + 1 tablespoon water, beaten
pearl sugar

## preparation

Dissolve yeast and sugar in warm water (110-115 degrees F.) Allow to stand until foamy, about 5 minutes.

Halve vanilla bean lengthwise and scrape out seeds. In a large bowl, combine yeast mixture, honey, melted butter, vanilla extract, vanilla seeds and eggs.

Add 1 1/2 cups of flour. With the paddle attachment of a heavy-duty mixer or by hand with a wooden spoon, beat mixture until very smooth. If using a heavy duty mixer, switch to the dough hook. If mixing by hand, continue with the wooden spoon. Gradually add as much of the remaining flour that is needed to make a very soft, bouncy dough. Turn dough out onto a moderately floured surface and knead until shiny. Place in a large oiled bowl, turn once to coat the top surface, and allow to rise until doubled in bulk, 30-40 minutes.

Preheat oven to Convect Bake 375 degrees F. Turn dough onto work surface and divide into two mounds. Divide each mound into three even pieces. Roll each piece into an

even rope about 14 inches long. Braid the ropes together, pinching the ends to seal.

Place loaves on on two parchment paper-lined baking sheets. Allow to rise in a warm place for 30 minutes.

Brush with egg glaze and sprinkle with pearl sugar. Bake for approximately 15-20 minutes, or until golden.

2 loaves.

# cranberry maple scones

Native Americans in what is now known as New England once called the syrup from the maple tree "sweetwater." Their pure maple syrup—the real stuff—is essential to this recipe..."pancake syrups" just won't do! This makes impressively tall, yet crumbly scones that are best eaten right out of the oven.

## ingredients

3 1/2 cups all purpose flour
1/2 cup whole wheat flour
1 cup quick-cooking oats, plus a little more for sprinkling
2 tablespoons baking powder
1/2 cup granulated sugar
1/2 cup chopped dried cranberries
2 teaspoons salt
2 sticks cold butter, each cut into 8 pieces
3/4 cup buttermilk
1/2 cup pure maple syrup
4 large eggs, lightly beaten
egg wash: 1 egg + 1 tablespoon water, beaten

maple icing:
1 1/4 cups powdered sugar
1/2 cup pure maple syrup
1 teaspoon pure vanilla extract

## preparation

Preheat oven to Convect Bake 350 degrees F.

In a mixing bowl of an electric mixer, combine all purpose flour, whole wheat flour, oats, baking powder, sugar, cranberries and salt. Stir well.

Add butter pieces and mix on low speed until butter is evenly distributed and mixture is coarse and crumbly.

In a small bowl, combine buttermilk, maple syrup and 4 eggs. Mix lightly. Add all at once to the flour mixture then mix just until the wet and dry ingredients begin to cling together.

Pour mixture into two oiled 8-inch pie dishes. Brush with egg wash and sprinkle with oats.

Convect Bake for 40-45 minutes, or until a pick inserted into the center comes out clean.

While scones are baking, combine icing ingredients and whisk until perfectly smooth. Cool scones slightly, then pour icing over the top.

Serve warm.

Serves 12.

# orange almond palmiers

These delicate pastries are wonderful for brunch. Palmiers—or palm leaves—are traditionally made with puff pastry dough, but we like this softer, less caloric yeast dough version.

ingredients

2 - 2 1/4 cups bread flour
1 1/2 teaspoons rapid rise yeast
3 tablespoons sugar
1/2 cup fresh orange juice
2 tablespoons butter, melted and cooled
1/2 teaspoon salt
1 egg
2/3 cup almond pie and pastry filling
2 teaspoons finely grated orange zest

preparation

Combine 2 cups of flour, yeast and sugar in the mixing bowl of a heavy duty mixer. Heat and stir orange juice, butter and salt in a small saucepan until quite warm (120-130 degrees F.) Add to flour mixture. Add egg. Beat at high speed for three minutes. Add additional flour if necessary, but for best results, dough should be quite soft.

Turn out onto a lightly floured board and knead until dough is smooth and elastic. Shape into a ball. Place in an oiled bowl, turning once. Cover with plastic wrap and allow to rise at room temperature until double in size (about 40 minutes.)

Turn dough onto a lightly floured surface. Cover and let rest 10 minutes. Roll dough into a 12 x 18 inch rectangle. Spread rectangle evenly with pie and pastry filling. Sprinkle with grated orange zest.

Beginning with one long edge, roll the dough, pinwheel style, to the center of the rectangle. Repeat with the other long edge, rolling it to the center to meet the other roll. With a sharp serrated knife, cut the roll evenly into 12 palmiers.

Lay palmiers filling side up on an oiled baking sheet. Allow to rise until almost double (approximately 1/2 hour.)

Preheat oven to Convect Bake 350 degrees F.

Bake palmiers for 15-18 minutes, until light golden brown.

Makes 12 palmiers.

Medallions of Roast Pork
with Honey Garlic Sauce
see page 26

# the main course

In restaurant vernacular, it's called the "center of the plate."

And the center is an important place.

The place where the eye, the nose and the palate join together in anticipation.

The place to develop your culinary style through your own interpretations of ingredients and techniques.

The place to showcase your talents by preparing luscious fish, perfectly broiled to moist perfection. To put forth the elegant simplicity of an exquisite roast chicken. To marry an extraordinary sauce with a handsome cut of meat, its delicious juices sealed within.

When you combine Jenn-Air Multi-Mode convection with your center of the plate creations, you'll be the one at the center.

The center of attention.

TIPS

When roasting chicken for four or more, try roasting two smaller hens rather than one large one. Two chickens will provide enough of both white and dark meat to please all, and any remaining chicken will make sandwiches, soup, or fill enchiladas the next day.

It is best not to salt meats before cooking. Salt draws liquid out of the tissue, resulting in dryness.

Use tongs when handling hot meats. Fork punctures drain meat of flavorful juices.

Add dried herbs at the beginning of the cooking, but fresh herbs in the last few minutes.

# medallions of roast pork with honey garlic sauce

(Photograph page 24)

### ingredients

1 pork tenderloin, (1 1/2 - 1 3/4 pounds)
1 tablespoon vegetable oil
2 tablespoons minced fresh garlic
1/2 cup soy sauce
1/4 cup honey
1 tablespoon minced orange zest
1/4 cup thick cut orange marmalade
1 tablespoon tomato catsup
non-stick spray

### preparation

In a small saucepan over medium heat, sauté garlic in vegetable oil until soft. Add soy sauce, honey, orange zest, marmalade, and tomato catsup. Whisk to blend. Bring to a boil, boil for 1 minute, then reduce to simmer. Simmer, uncovered, for 12-15 minutes.  Set aside.

Spray broiler pan with non-stick spray.  Place tenderloin on pan. Convect Roast at 375 degrees F. for 30-35 minutes, or until internal temperature registers 160 F.  Allow the pork tenderloin to rest at room temperature for 8-10 minutes.

Slice pork into 1/2 inch thick medallions.  Arrange on serving plates and serve with Honey Garlic Sauce.

Serves 6.

# almond crumb salmon

### ingredients

1/2 cup fresh bread crumbs
1/4 cup finely chopped fresh flat-leaf parsley
1/2 cup sliced almonds
2 teaspoons Italian seasoning
1/2  teaspoon salt
1/4 teaspoon freshly ground pepper
2 egg whites
6  4-ounce salmon filets

### preparation

Line a baking sheet with parchment paper.

In a shallow bowl or pie dish, combine bread crumbs, parsley, almonds, Italian seasoning, salt and pepper. Toss well.

In a shallow bowl or pie dish, whisk egg whites with fork until light and frothy.

Dip flesh side of salmon filet into egg white and then dredge in almond mixture. Pat almond mixture into salmon with fingers. Place skin-side down on parchment-lined baking sheet. Repeat, using all salmon filets. Sprinkle any leftover almond fixture over the top of the filets.

Convect Roast at 425 degrees F. for 15-25 minutes, (approximately 8-9 minutes per inch of thickness) or until salmon flakes with fork.

Serve immediately.

Serves 6.

*Almond Crumb Salmon*

*Chicken Roast with Herb Butter*

# chicken roast with herb butter

*Poultry is for the cook what canvas is to the painter.*
Brillat-Savarin

### ingredients

1 3-4 pound roasting chicken
salt and pepper, to taste
6 tablespoons butter at room temperature
1 cup chopped fresh parsley
1/2 cup chopped fresh chives
2 tablespoons chopped fresh rosemary
2 tablespoons chopped fresh thyme
2 tablespoons chopped fresh sage
3 tablespoons extra virgin olive oil

### preparation

Rinse the chicken and pat dry. Sprinkle the cavity with salt and pepper.

In a processor, blend the butter and herbs to make a paste. Carefully lift the skin from the breast of the chicken and spread the butter mixture between the skin and the flesh. Smooth out the skin and hold in place with tooth-picks. Rub the olive oil over the chicken and sprinkle with salt and pepper.

Convect Roast at 375 degrees F. for 1 1/2 hours or until inter-nal temperature is 170-180 F. Let rest at room temperature for 10 minutes before carving.

Serves 4.

# upscale meatloaf with sundried tomatoes, basil and smoked mozzarella

*(adapted with gratitude from a recipe by Julee Rosso & Sheila Lukins)*

This is comfort food, elevated. It is marvelous served hot, with mashed potatoes in the winter. In warmer months, it is superlative cold, served thinly sliced, with salads and picnic fare. This recipe makes two loaf pans.

## ingredients

2 pounds ground round (95% lean)
1 pound sweet Italian sausage, sautéed until no longer pink
   and well drained
1 medium onion, chopped
4 cloves of garlic, minced
3 cups fresh bread crumbs (do not use dry)
1/2 cup chopped Italian parsley
2 tablespoons Italian herb seasoning
salt and freshly ground pepper, to taste
2 eggs, lightly beaten
1/2 cup tomato puree
1/2 cup dry red wine
1 cup fresh basil leaves
4 ounces sun-dried tomatoes, oil packed, drained
   and chopped
1 pound smoked mozzarella, thinly sliced

## preparation

Preheat oven to Convect Bake 375 degrees F.

In a large bowl, combine ground round, cooked Italian sausage, onion, garlic, bread crumbs, parsley, Italian seasoning, salt and pepper. Mix well, preferably with your hands. Add the eggs, tomato puree and wine.

Oil 2 standard loaf pans. Divide 1/3 of the meat mixture between the pans. Divide 1/2 of the fresh basil between the pans, pressing it into the meat mixture. Divide 1/2 of the sundried tomatoes between the pans, sprinkling them over the basil. Divide 1/2 of the mozzarella between the pans, arranging it over the sundried tomatoes. Divide 1/3 of the meat mixture between the pans. Repeat, ending with final 1/3 of meat mixture.

Convect Bake for 45-50 minutes. Cool 10 minutes before slicing.

Serves 12.

# yellowfin tuna with mango avocado salsa

If you can't find fresh mango, look for jars of mango slices, usually available refrigerated in the produce section of your market. This sassy salsa is also terrific on grilled chicken, on sandwiches or tossed with greens for a refreshing salad.

## ingredients

salsa:

2 fresh mangos, peeled, seeded and chopped
1 cup chopped red bell pepper
3 tablespoons finely chopped fresh cilantro
1/3 cup finely chopped fresh red onion
2 tablespoons white wine vinegar
1 tablespoon extra virgin olive oil
1 tablespoon sugar
1/2 teaspoon salt
1 ripe avocado, cubed

tuna:

4 6-ounce tuna steaks
2 tablespoons white wine vinegar
1 tablespoon sugar
1 tablespoon extra virgin olive oil
salt and pepper to taste

## preparation

In a non-metal bowl combine chopped mangoes, bell pepper, cilantro, red onion, white wine vinegar, sugar, salt, and 1 table-spoon extra virgin olive oil. Refrigerate for 30 minutes. (salsa may be prepared one day ahead and refrigerated.)

Place oven rack in top position. Place tuna steaks on oiled broiler pan.

Sprinkle with salt and pepper. Combine remaining vinegar, sugar and oil in a small bowl, then drizzle over tuna steaks.

Convect Broil on HI for 10-12 minutes per inch of thickness, turning halfway through. While tuna is broiling, peel, seed and cube avocado. Add to salsa mixture; stir to blend. Serve over hot tuna steaks.

Serves 4.

# chicken havana

Do not let this list of seemingly incompatible ingredients deter you from making this incredibly flavorful dish. It is a dish you will become famous for; a dish that will rise to the top of your repertoire.

### ingredients

4 chicken breast halves
4 chicken thighs
2 tablespoons finely minced garlic
1/4 cup dried oregano
salt and pepper to taste
1/2 cup red wine vinegar
1/2 cup extra virgin olive oil
1 cup currants*
1 cup pitted Spanish olives, whole
1/2 cup capers
6 bay leaves
1/2 cup brown sugar
1/2 cup dry white wine
chopped cilantro

* raisins or pitted prunes may also be used

### preparation

In a large non-metal bowl or large zipping plastic bag, combine chicken, garlic, oregano, salt and pepper, vinegar, olive oil, currants, olives, capers and bay leaves. Seal and let marinate, refrigerated, 12 hours.

Arrange chicken in a 9x13 inch baking dish. Spoon the marinade over the chicken. Sprinkle chicken pieces with brown sugar and carefully pour wine into the bottom of the pan.

Convect Roast at 350 degrees F. for 55-60 minutes, or until a meat thermometer Inserted into the thickest part of the chicken pieces registers 170 degrees F. Arrange on serving platter, sprinkle with chopped cilantro and pass pan juices in a sauceboat.

Serves 4-6.

# latin lime flank steak with raspberry salsa

Once regarded as one of the "poor cousin" cuts of beef, flank steak has now become a most fashionable cut. And rightly so... flank steak is lean, it has a full-bodied beef flavor and it cooks quickly.

### ingredients

steak:
1-2 1/2 pound flank steak
juice of one lime (1/4 cup)
1 teaspoon finely minced garlic
1 tablespoon ground cumin
1 tablespoon chili powder
1 teaspoon coriander
1 1/2 teaspoon hot pepper flakes
salt to taste

raspberry salsa:
1/2 cup cranberry/raspberry juice concentrate
zest of 1 lime
juice of 1 lime (1/4 cup)
1 pint fresh raspberries
1/2 medium red onion, finely chopped
2 tablespoons chopped fresh cilantro
1/2 fresh jalapeno, minced

### preparation

Spray broiler pan with non-stick cooking spray. Squeeze lime juice over both sides of flank steak and rub into grain. Rub minced garlic into grain. Place steak on broiler pan.

In a small bowl, combine cumin, chili powder, coriander, salt and hot pepper flakes. Rub this mixture over the steak and into the grain. Let stand while you make raspberry salsa.

To make salsa, combine all ingredients in a large bowl. Mash lightly with a fork.

Convect Broil flank steak on HI for 8-10 minutes, turning halfway through, until steak is medium rare (145 degrees F.). Do not overcook! Let rest at room temperature for 5 minutes, then slice across the grain and serve with raspberry salsa.

Serves 6.

Roasted Summer Vegetables
see page 34

# vegetables and side dishes

They're the perfect accessories.

The ones to dress up that perfect, little black dress of an entrée you've planned for the evening meal.

Gorgeous grains and vibrant vegetables. The first asparagus of spring. The aromatic summer tomatoes. The rustic squashes that usher us from fall to winter. The herb scented pilafs, the cream enriched potatoes.

The Jenn-Air Multi-Mode Convection Oven treats them like the gems that they are.

And assures you that all of your meals will be perfectly attired.

TIPS

When roasting vegetables, pan size is important. Vegetables should fit in a single layer. If they are too thin, the vegetable juices will burn. If they are too thick, vegetables will steam instead of roast.

Coat vegetables very lightly with a coating of fat such as olive oil or butter. The coating will seal in the vegetables' moisture and will promote even browning.

Unfortunately, many modern pesticides concentrate in vegetable skin and cannot be removed by washing in water. Peeling vegetables safeguards against contamination.

Hydroponically grown vegetables—vegetables grown in nutrient-rich water instead of in soil, are some of the most beautiful to look at, but often lack the intense flavors found in those that grow in the ground.

When it comes to vegetables, bigger is not better. Actually, the younger and smaller the vegetable, the more tender and sweet it will be.

# roasted summer vegetables

(Photograph page 32)

*Do vegetarians eat animal crackers?*
Anonymous

## ingredients

3 tablespoons extra virgin olive oil
4 medium tomatoes, peeled and halved
1 medium zucchini, cut into 4 pieces
2 yellow bell peppers, quartered and seeded
4 large mushrooms, halved
1/2 head garlic, broken into cloves and peeled
1 teaspoon finely chopped fresh marjoram
1 teaspoon finely chopped fresh thyme
1 bunch fresh asparagus tips
salt and freshly ground black pepper

## preparation

Spread half of the olive oil over the bottom of a roasting pan or baking sheet with 1-inch sides.

Cut the tomatoes in half and squeeze out their seeds. Place on baking dish along with zucchini, bell peppers, mushrooms and garlic. Sprinkle with marjoram and thyme. Drizzle with remaining olive oil. Toss to distribute oil. Convect Roast at 375 degrees F. for 30-35 minutes. Remove from oven. Add asparagus tips, toss lightly and return to oven for an additional 5-7 minutes.

Season to taste with salt and pepper. Serve hot or at room temperature.

Serves 4.

# new potatoes roasted in salt

*Salt is born of the purest of parents, the sun and the sea.*
Pythagoras

## ingredients

2 teaspoons minced fresh garlic
2 tablespoons extra virgin olive oil for dish plus 2 tablespoons for drizzling
3 tablespoons fresh whole rosemary leaves
30 small new potatoes, scrubbed
1 1/2 pounds kosher salt
1/4 cup all purpose flour
1/2 cup water

## preparation

Mix the minced garlic and 2 tablespoons of olive oil together and spread on the bottom of a 10-12 inch gratin dish or 9x13 inch baking pan. Sprinkle with rosemary leaves. Place the potatoes close together on top.

In a large bowl, combine the salt and the flour. Mix well. Slowly stir in 1/2 cup of water and mix until well combined.

Pour the salt mixture over the top of the potatoes and spread evenly, filling all of the spaces between the potatoes.

Convect Roast at 450 degrees F. for 40-50 minutes or until poatoes are tender when pierced with a fork. Remove from oven, cool for 5 minutes, then invert pan onto serving platter. Drizzle potatoes with additional olive oil and garnish with several grinding of fresh black pepper.

Serves 6.

*New Potatoes Roasted in Salt*

*Tuscan Roasted Green Beans*

# tuscan roasted green beans

Anchovy paste is a combination of mashed anchovies, vinegar, spices and water.

### ingredients

1 pound fresh green beans, stems trimmed
1/4 cup extra virgin olive oil
2 large cloves of garlic, minced
1 tablespoon chopped fresh summer savory
1 tablespoon anchovy paste
1 tablespoon finely grated lemon zest
1 tablespoon fresh lemon juice
salt and freshly ground pepper to taste

### preparation

Toss the beans, olive oil, garlic and savory together on an Baking sheet. Spread the beans out in an even layer.

Convect Roast at 425 degrees F. for 30-35 minutes, or until barely tender. Transfer the beans to a large bowl.

In a small bowl, whisk together anchovy paste, lemon zest, lemon juice and salt and pepper to taste. Drizzle over warm green beans and toss well to coat. Serve warm.

Serves 4.

# sherried root vegetables

### ingredients

1/2 cup extra virgin olive oil
1/2 cup dry Sherry
2 teaspoons sea salt
2 teaspoons freshly ground pepper
6 sprigs of fresh thyme
6 sprigs of rosemary
6 sprigs of fresh savory
6 large carrots, peeled and cut into bite-sized pieces
  halved lengthwise
6 parsnips, peeled and cut into bite-sized pieces
  halved lengthwise
6 small leeks, halved lengthwise and cut into
  bite-sized pieces
3 red onions, peeled and cut into bite-sized pieces
12 small new red potatoes
6 shallots, peeled and cut in half
6 green onions, chopped
2 heads of garlic (about 18 cloves,) peeled and cut in half

### preparation

In a large bowl, mix together the olive oil, Sherry, salt, pepper, thyme, rosemary and savory. Add all of the vegetables and turn them until they are well coated with the olive oil mixture. With a slotted spoon, remove all of the vegetables except for the green onions and arrange in a single layer in a large roasting pan. Reserve the oil mixture.

Convect Roast at 400 degrees F. for 30 minutes. Baste vegetables with reserved olive oil mixture and add green onions. Continue roasting until vegetables are tender, about 20 minutes longer.

Serve hot or at room temperature.

Serves 6.

# sweet potato fries with garlic and herbs

### ingredients

1 1/2 pounds sweet potatoes, peeled and cut into French
  fry-style strips
1 teaspoon minced garlic
2 tablespoons extra-virgin olive oil
2 tablespoons chopped flat-leaf parsley
1 teaspoon chopped fresh thyme
1 teaspoon kosher salt

### preparation

Spray two oven-proof cooling racks with non-stick spray.
Place the racks over two baking sheets.

In a large bowl, toss sweet potato strips with olive oil and
garlic. Spread potatoes on the cooling rack in a single layer.

Convect roast at 425 degrees F. until tender and golden
brown, about 15-18 minutes.

Transfer to serving platter. Sprinkle with salt, parsley and
thyme. Serve immediately.

Serves 4.

Chocolate Truffle Torte
see page 42

# sweets

Dessert.

The last course to be placed upon the table, but the one that lingers the longest in memory: the course by which the rest of the meal is judged.

Definitely not a place to depend on an ordinary oven.

You need an oven that respects what you put into it.

An oven that promises you consistent, delicious results.

The Jenn-Air Multi-Mode Convection Oven.

With Jenn-Air Multi-Mode convection, you will bake remarkable desserts—silky crèmes brulèe, rich bread puddings, dense chocolate tortes, flaky pies and sweet surprises dressed in a tailored cloak of puff pastry.

Desserts they will remember.

From a cook they won't forget.

## TIPS

When choosing fruits for poaching, pick ones that are a day or two short of perfect ripeness. Overly ripe fruits tend to become too mushy. The perfect poaching fruit will dent at the stem end when pressed with a fingertip.

Desserts will only be as good as the ingredients that go into them:
- *Margarine is vastly inferior to butter. You may substitute if you must, but texture and flavor will not be the same.*
- *Pure vanilla extract is best. If you must pinch pennies, follow this rule: use imitation vanilla in products that are baked; use pure vanilla in products that are not.*

- *The price of chocolate is usually indicative of its quality. The baking chocolates commonly found on American grocery shelves are acceptable, but specialty chocolates, such as Lindt, Valhrona and Callebaut, are superb.*

No matter what your Home Ec teacher said, you do not have to sift flour. The following recipes, as well as many others, will turn out perfectly with the spoon and scrape method. Simply spoon flour into the measuring cup and scrape any excess from the top of the cup with the straight edge of a knife.

For best performance, separate eggs when chilled, but bring them to room temperature before adding to batters or dough.

# sourdough bread pudding with white chocolate and mixed berries

*Sweets to the sweet.*
William Shakespeare

### ingredients

3 cups sourdough bread, torn into small pieces
2 cups half and half
4 ounces white chocolate, chopped
1 egg
4 egg yolks
1/4 cup granulated sugar
1 teaspoon vanilla
1/2 teaspoon almond extract

white chocolate sauce:
3/4 cup whipping cream
4 ounces white chocolate, finely chopped
1 pint assorted fresh berries - strawberries, raspberries, blackberries, blueberries

### preparation

Preheat oven to Convect Bake 350 degrees F.

Butter an 8-9 inch glass pie dish. Place the torn bread in the dish.

In a medium saucepan, heat the half and half until hot, but not boiling. Add 4 ounces of chopped white chocolate and stir until chocolate is melted. Cool slightly.

In a medium bowl, beat egg, egg yolks and sugar until well blended. Whisk in the warm white chocolate and cream mixture, vanilla and almond extract. Pour over bread pieces and bake 30-35 minutes. Set aside to cool while you prepare sauce.

To make sauce, heat whipping cream until hot, but not boiling. Add 4 ounces of white chocolate and stir until chocolate is melted.

Cut bread pudding into wedges and serve with fresh berries and white chocolate sauce.

Serves 8.

# ricotta and pine nut tart with balsamic strawberries

### ingredients

Pastry crust:
2 cups all-purpose flour
1/2 cups sugar
1/3 cups pine nuts, toasted and finely chopped
3/4 cup unsalted butter, melted

Filling:
1 1/2 cups sugar
1 cup water
6 ounces cream cheese, softened
1 cup ricotta cheese
3 egg yolks
2 whole eggs
1/4 cup pine nuts, whole

Balsamic Strawberries:
2 pints fresh strawberries
2 tablespoons sugar
1 tablespoon top quality Balsamic vinegar

### preparation

Pastry Crust:
Preheat oven to Convect Bake 350 degrees F.

In a small bowl, mix flour, sugar and chopped pine nuts. Add melted butter and mix gently.

Press mixture into bottom and about 1 inch up the sides of a 10-inch spring form pan. Chill for ten minutes. Place aluminum foil over the pastry and fill with pie weights, dry beans or rice. Convect Bake for 15 minutes. Remove foil and pie weights, then bake an additional 10 minutes, or until golden brown. Cool completely.

Filling:
In a small saucepan, bring water and sugar to a boil. Boil until sugar is completely dissolved, about 4 minutes. Set aside.

In a food processor, blend cream cheese, ricotta cheese, egg yolks and whole eggs. Blend well. With the machine still running, add the sugar syrup slowly.

Pour the cheese mixture into the prepared crust. Sprinkle the whole pine nuts over the top. Return to oven and Convect Bake the tart for 40-45 minutes, or until golden but still a bit soft in the middle.

Cool.  Serve topped with Balsamic Strawberries.

Balsamic Strawberries:
Clean the strawberries by wiping them with a damp paper towel, one by one. (Washing in water will dilute the flavor.)

Hull and slice strawberries. Place in a shallow pan and sprinkle with sugar. Cover tightly with plastic wrap. Allow to stand at room temperature for 30 minutes. Shake occasionally.

Sprinkle with balsamic vinegar, shake pan to distribute flavor and allow to stand at room temperature for 30 more minutes.

Serves 8.

# chocolate truffle torte

(Photograph page 38)

*An intensely chocolate dessert will activate any endorphin known to man.*
Grant Showly

ingredients
cake:
1/2 cup butter
1/2 cup corn syrup
1 cup semisweet chocolate chips
1/2 cup granulated sugar
3 large eggs
1 teaspoon pure vanilla extract
1 cup flour
pinch salt

glaze:
4 ounces unsweetened chocolate
4 ounces sweet chocolate (like German's)
8 tablespoons butter, softened
1/4 cup light corn syrup

preparation
Preheat oven to Convect Bake 350 degrees F.

Butter and flour a 9-inch round cake pan.

In a medium saucepan, heat butter and corn syrup over low heat, stirring frequently, until butter is melted. Stir in chocolate chips and continue to stir over low heat until chocolate chips are melted. Remove pan from heat; stir in vanilla and flour. Mix until well blended and smooth. Stir in sugar and eggs. Mix well.

Pour batter into prepared pan and bake 20-25 minutes, or until center springs back when pressed lightly with finger.

Cool for ten minutes then turn out onto cooling rack. Cool torte completely.

In a small saucepan, melt chocolates over very low heat, stirring constantly. Stir until almost melted, then remove from heat and stir until melted and smooth. Stir in the butter 1 tablespoon at a time. Stir in corn syrup. Pour over the torte, allowing the glaze to coat the sides. Refrigerate until glaze is set.

Serves 8-10.

# macadamia shortbread with lime marmalade

Serves 6-8.

## ingredients

3/4 cup unsalted butter
1/2 cup brown sugar
1/2 teaspoon pure vanilla extract
1 1/2 cups all-purpose flour
1/8 teaspoon salt
1/2 cup finely chopped macadamia nuts
1/4 cup lime marmalade

## preparation

Preheat oven to Convect Bake 350 degrees F.

Beat butter and brown sugar on medium speed for 3-4 minutes or until very light and fluffy. Scrape down the sides of the bowl and beat an additional minute. Add vanilla extract and stir to combine.

In a small bowl, combine flour, salt and 1/4 cup of the macadamia nuts. Add to the butter mixture and beat on low speed just to combine, for about a minute. Dough will be very stiff. Remove 1/2 cup of dough, spread it in a thin layer on a plate and place it in the freezer for approximately 10 minutes.

Using fingers, press remaining dough into bottom of a 9-inch spring form pan. Spread marmalade evenly over the dough to within 1 inch of the edge. Remove remaining dough from the freezer and crumble over the marmalade, allowing some of marmalade to show through. Sprinkle remaining macadamia nuts over the top.

Convect Bake for 24-26 minutes, until golden brown. Cool on rack, and then remove from pan. Cut into wedges and sprinkle with powdered sugar.

# lemon créme brûlée

Ingredients

2 cups heavy cream
1/4 cup finely grated lemon zest
3 large eggs
2 large egg yolks
1/3 cup sugar
1/4 cup fresh lemon juice
pinch of salt
1/2 cup sugar

preparation

Position rack in the middle of the oven and preheat to Convect Bake 325 degrees F. Bring a kettle of water to a boil. Place six 5-ounce crème brûlée dishes in the bottom of a large roasting pan.

In a small saucepan over medium heat bring cream and lemon zest to a simmer. Remove the pan from the heat, cover and allow to stand for 10 minutes.

In a medium bowl, combine eggs, yolks, 1/3 cup sugar, lemon juice and salt. Whisk lightly to combine. Add 1/2 of the cream mixture, stirring gently with a wooden spoon to avoid creating air bubbles. In a slow, steady stream, pour in the remaining cream, stirring constantly.

Pour the custard through a fine mesh sieve into a 4-cup glass measuring cup. Using the cup, carefully pour custard into crème brûlée dishes. Fill bottom of pan with boiling water, halfway up sides of the dishes.

Convect Bake for 20-25 minutes, or until just set around the edges but a bit jiggly in the center. Remove dishes from pan and chill for at least 6 hours or overnight.

Remove from refrigerator. Preheat broiler to HI. Gently blot tops of custards with the corner of a paper towel to absorb surface moisture. Sprinkle each custard evenly with 1-2 tablespoons of sugar. Place under broiler until sugar melts and browns. Serve immediately.

Serves 6.

# zinfandel pears in puff pastry

(Photograph on front cover)

### ingredients

3 cups Zinfandel wine
3 cups sugar
2 1/2 cups water
4 whole cloves
2 teaspoons pure vanilla extract
2 cups freshly squeezed orange juice
2 cinnamon sticks
8 black peppercorns
12 firm, but ripe Bosc pears
1 pound frozen puff pastry dough, thawed

egg glaze:
1 egg + 1 tablespoon water, beaten

### preparation

In a large saucepan, combine Zinfandel, sugar, water, cloves, vanilla, orange juice, cinnamon sticks and peppercorns. Bring to a boil, reduce heat and simmer until sugar dissolves completely.

Carefully peel pears. Core carefully from the bottom, being careful not to break pears. Place pears in Zinfandel mixture. Cover pan, bring to a simmer and poach pears for 20-25 minutes, or until pears pierce easily with a knife. Remove pears from the liquid and refrigerate until cool.

Bring pear poaching liquid to a boil and allow to reduce over medium-high heat until the mixture thickens to the consistency of pancake syrup. Strain through a fine mesh colander and set aside.

On a lightly floured work surface, roll a sheet of puff pastry into an 8 x 14 inch rectangle. Using a fluted pastry wheel, cut pastry into 1/2 inch x 8 inch strips.

Preheat oven to Convect Bake 375 degrees F. Place the end of one pastry strip under a pear. Starting at the bottom, wrap the pear with the strip and add more lengths of pastry as needed, joining strips together with egg glaze. Press the end of the strip against the top of the pear. Repeat with all of the pears. Brush pears with egg glaze.

Convect Bake pears until puff pastry is golden brown, for 18-22 minutes. Allow pears to cool to room temperature.

To serve, ladle thickened poaching syrup on dessert plates or bowls. Place pears on top. Serve at room temperature.

Serves 6.

Rack of Lamb with Kiwi Mint Sauce
see page 51

# entertaining

One friend treating other friends.

To conversation, to companionship, to the very best from your kitchen.

Dishes that show off your culinary panache. Foods that make them ooh and ahh. Luxurious chops of spring lamb with young shoots of asparagus. Robust beef tenderloin jazzed up with notes of citrus. Steaming concoctions of pasta and cheese.

Easier said than done, some people would say.

But not you. You know better. You know that the best dinner parties are personal, relaxed and expressive. A gift from you to them.

And you know that your Jenn-Air Multi-Mode Convection Oven will help you keep them that way.

TIPS

As you learn your friends' favorite foods and flavors, make note of them in a small book reserved for that purpose. Then, when you invite them to dinner, you can surprise them with their favorite foods.

The best way to make guests comfortable is to bring them into the kitchen. The kitchen is a warm, easy place; a guaranteed ice breaker.

Come to terms with the fact that you cannot please all of the people all of the time, especially when it comes to food.

When preparing a meal or hors d'oeurve for a large group, prepare dishes that please you.

Make sure that the fragrance of the flowers you choose does not compete with the aromas of the food you prepare.

Always consider your refrigerator space before you plan a menu. Can you find room for the big salad bowl? Is there room for the wine? If not, make early arrangements for rentals.

# lasagne with shrimp, scallops and snow crab

(Photograph page 4)

*The trouble with eating Italian food is that five or six days later you're hungry again.*
George Miller

## ingredients

sauce:
3 tablespoons extra virgin olive oil
1 medium yellow onion, chopped
4 cloves garlic, minced
2 24-ounce cans of plum tomatoes packed in puree
1/2 cup dry white wine
1/2 cup chopped fresh basil
1 teaspoon fennel seeds
salt and pepper to taste
1 cup half and half
12 ounces peeled and deveined shrimp, poached just
   until opaque
12 ounces scallops, poached just until opaque
1 pound lasagne noodles, fresh or fresh frozen

filling:
4 cups ricotta cheese
8 ounces cream cheese, softened
2 eggs
1 10-ounce package frozen spinach, thawed and
   squeezed dry
1 pound frozen snow crab meat, thawed according to
   package directions
1 sweet red pepper, diced
1 bunch of scallions, chopped
1/2 cup chopped fresh basil

salt and pepper to taste
1 1/2 pounds grated mozzarella cheese

## preparation

To make sauce, heat oil in large skillet. Add onion and garlic; saute for 5 minutes. Add tomatoes with puree and simmer another 5 minutes. Stir in the wine, basil, fennel seeds, salt and pepper. Simmer, stirring occasionally, for 30 minutes. Stir the half & half, shrimp and scallops into the sauce. Remove from heat.

Preheat oven to Convect Bake 350 degrees F.

To make filling, combine ricotta cheese, cream cheese and eggs; beat until smooth. Stir in spinach, crab meat, red pepper, scallions, basil and salt and pepper to taste.

In an oiled 10x14 inch roasting pan or lasagna pan, spread 1/3 cup of the sauce over the bottom. Cover with a layer of the noodles. Top with half of the filling, then half of the sauce. Cover the sauce with half of the mozzarella. Add another layer of noodles, the remaining half of the filling. Top with remaining mozzarella and remaining sauce. Cover with remaining cheese.

Bake the lasagne for 50-55 minutes. Allow to stand 10 minutes before cutting into portions.

Serves 10-12.

# chicken wellington with champagne sauce

(Photograph on back cover)

*Come quickly! I am drinking stars.*
Dom Perignon, upon tasting his first bottle of champagne

### ingredients

4 skinless, boneless chicken breast halves
10 ounce package frozen chopped spinach, thawed
  and squeezed dry
2 tablespoons butter
1/3 cup chopped green onions
2 cloves of garlic, minced
4 ounces dried morel mushrooms, soaked in warm water
  for 1 hour, drained and chopped
3/4 cup dry white wine
1 tablespoon chopped fresh thyme
1  17-ounce package frozen puff pastry (2 sheets) thawed
1 egg beaten to blend with 1 tablespoon water (for glaze)

champagne sauce:
1 tablespoon butter
1/4 cup finely chopped green onions
1 tablespoon all-purpose flour
1 1/4 cup reduced sodium chicken broth
1 1/4 cup good quality champagne

### preparation

Preheat oven to Convect Broil on HI.

Spray broiler pan with non-stick cooking spray. Arrange
chicken breast halves on broiler pan. Season to taste with
salt and freshly ground pepper.

Broil until almost cooked through, for approximately 4-5
minutes per side.

Preheat oven to Convect Bake 375 degrees F.

Melt butter in a large skillet. Add green onions and garlic;
saute until tender, about 3 minutes. Add morel mushrooms
and saute another 2 minutes. Add wine and thyme; simmer
until most of the liquid in the pan evaporates, approximately
6 minutes. Remove from heat, season with salt and pepper
to taste and cool.

Roll puff pastry sheets into 12-inch squares on a lightly
floured surface. Cut each square in half crosswise to create
four 12 x 6 inch rectangles.

Place 1 chicken breast crosswise at one of the short ends
of each rectangle. Divide spinach evenly over the top of
each chicken breast. Top each with 1/4 of the morel mush-
room mixture. Roll up like a jelly-roll, pinching edges to seal.
Place seam side down on an oiled baking tray.

Bake pastries until puffed and golden brown, approximately
20-25 minutes. Serve immediately with Champagne
Sauce. Ladle sauce onto plate, place pastry on top.

Champagne Sauce:
Melt butter in a medium saucepan over medium-high heat.
Add chopped green onions and sauté until golden.
Add flour, stir until bubbly and golden, about 3 minutes.
Add chicken broth and champagne; simmer, whisking
frequently, for about 15 minutes, or until sauce reduces to
desired consistency.

Serves 4.

# tenderloin of beef with three citrus sauce

### ingredients

Marinade:

1/3 cup soy sauce
1/4 cup red wine
1/4 cup chopped onion
2 tablespoons dark brown sugar
3 tablespoons fresh lime juice
1/4 teaspoon hot pepper sauce
1 clove garlic, minced
2 1/2 pounds beef tenderloin, in one piece, trimmed
    and tied

Citrus Sauce:

2 tablespoons reserved marinade
2 oranges, pith removed, chopped
1/4 lemon, pith removed, chopped
1/2 grapefruit, pith removed, chopped
1/4 cup chopped green onion
2 tablespoons sugar
2 tablespoons chopped fresh cilantro
2 tablespoons orange juice
2 tablespoons rice vinegar

### preparation

Marinade:

Combine soy sauce, red wine, onion, brown sugar, lime juice, hot pepper sauce and garlic in a gallon-size zipping plastic bag. Shake to combine. Remove 2 tablespoons of marinade; set aside. Add beef tenderloin; close bag and refrigerate for 2-4 hours.

Citrus Sauce:

Combine all ingredients in a non-metal bowl. Allow to stand at room temperature for 2 hours.

Remove tenderloin from marinade and place on rack in roasting pan. Discard marinade.

Convect Roast at 425 degrees F. for 45-50 minutes, for medium rare or until desired temperature is reached. Allow to stand, loosely covered with foil, for 10 minutes. Slice into 1/2 inch slices and serve with Citrus Sauce.

Serves 8.

# rack of lamb with kiwi mint sauce

(Photograph page 46)

ingredients

1/2 cup sugar
1/3 cup raspberry vinegar
1/3 cup fresh lime juice
2 cups chopped fresh mint leaves
4 kiwis, peeled and diced
1 tablespoon finely grated lime zest
2 racks of lamb with 7 bones each(approximately 1 1/2
   pounds each) frenched
3 tablespoons Dijon mustard
2 cloves garlic, minced
1/2 teaspoon freshly ground pepper
2 teaspoons chopped fresh thyme
1/2 cup chopped fresh parsley
2 cups fresh bread crumbs
1/2 cup melted butter

preparation

In a small saucepan, combine sugar, raspberry vinegar and lime juice. Bring to a boil, reduce heat to low and simmer for 5 minutes. Remove from heat and cool to room temperature. When cool, add mint, kiwi and lime zest. Chill until serving time.

Place racks in a roasting pan. Convect Roast at 400 degrees F. for 20 minutes. Remove from oven and cool slightly.

Brush cooled lamb with Dijon mustard, sprinkle with minced garlic, pepper and thyme. In a small bowl, combine parsley, bread crumbs and melted butter. Coat meat generously with crumb mixture.

Return lamb to oven and roast approximately 20 minutes longer for medium rare (145 degrees F.). Remove from oven, cover loosely with foil and allow to stand for 5 minutes before cutting.

Cut rack into chops. Arrange 2 chops and kiwi mint salsa on each plate. Serve immediately.

Serves 6.

# Convection Roasting times and temperatures for vegetables

Note: It is impossible to give exact times and temperatures for roasting vegetables because they will cook differently depending on their age and size. Vegetables should be arranged in single layer. For best results coat lightly with olive oil. Times are based on no preheat.

| VEGETABLE | Temperature Range (degrees F) | Conventional Time (min) | Convection Time (min) |
|---|---|---|---|
| Asparagus | 400-425 | 15-20 | 10-15 |
| Beets | 400-425 | 90-100, large beets | 70-80, large beets |
|  |  | 60-70, baby beets | 50-60, small beets |
| Carrots | 375-400 | 50 | 35–40 |
| Garlic, whole head | 375-400 | 90 | 60-70 |
| Mushrooms | 400-425 | 20 | 15-20 |
| Onions | 400-425 | 40, small onions | 30-40, small onions |
|  |  | 90, large onions | 70-80, large onions |
| Potatoes | 400-425 | 60-65, quartered | 45-55, quartered |
|  |  | 35-40 baby potatoes | 35-40 baby potatoes |
| Sweet Potatoes | 375-400 | 50 | 30-40 |
| Tomatoes | 400-425: large tomatoes | 180 | 50-60 |
|  | 300-325: cherry tomatoes | 120 | 40-50 |
| Zucchini | 350-375 | 40-45 | 35-40 |
| Eggplant | 425-450 | 25-30, sliced | 20-25, sliced |

# Convection Roasting times and temperatures for meats

Note: Roasting times are based on meats at refrigerator temperatures and no preheat.

| BEEF (Roasted to 150F) | Temperature (degrees F) | Conventional Time (min/lb) | Convection Time (min/lb) |
|---|---|---|---|
| Rib Eye Roast, 3-4 lbs | 350 | 30-35 | 20-30 |
| Standing Rib Roast, 2-3 lb. | 325 | 30-35 | 20-30 |
| Tenderloin Roast, 2-3 lb. | 400 | 20-30 | 15-25 |
| **POULTRY (Roasted to 170 F in the Breast)** | | | |
| Chicken, whole, 2 1/2 – 3 1/2 lb. | 375 | 20-25 | 15-22 |
| Turkey breast, boneless 3 lb. | 325 | 30-40 | 25-35 |
| Turkey, whole, 12-16 lb. | 325 | 18-20 | 12-16 |
| **PORK (Roasted to 160 F)** | | | |
| Pork Loin Roast, boneless, 2-3 lb. | 325 | 25-30 | 20-25 |
| Tenderloin Roast, 1-2 lb. | 325 | 25-30 | 20-30 |
| **LAMB (Roasted to 160 F)** | | | |
| Leg, boneless, 2-3lb | 325 | 35-40 | 30-35 |
| Leg, whole, 5-7 lb. | 325 | 30-35 | 25-30 |

# Drying Guide

**FRUITS**

|  | Apples* | Apricots* | Bananas* | Cherries | Nectarines and Peaches* | Pears* |
|---|---|---|---|---|---|---|
| **Varieties Best for Drying** | Firm varieties: Graven Stein, Granny Smith, Jonathan, Winesap, Rome Beauty, Newton | Blenheim/Royal most common, Tilton also good | Firm varieties | Lambert, Royal Ann, Napoleon, Van or Bing | Freestone varieties | Bartlett |
| **Preparation** | Wash, peel if desired, core and slice into 1/8" slices. | Wash, halve, and remove pits. | Peel and cut into 1/4" slices | Wash and remove stems. Halve and remove pits. | Halve and remove pits. Peeling is optional but results in better-looking dried fruit | Peel, halve and core |
| **Approx. DryingTime at 140°F** | 4-8 hours | 18-24 hours | 17-24 hours | 18-24 hours | 24-36 hours | 24-36 hours |
| **Test for Doneness** | Pilable to crisp. Dried apples store best when they are slightly crisp. | Soft, pliable. | Pilable to crisp. | Pliable and leathery. | Pliable and leathery. | Soft and pliable. |